Freya - Goddess Of Opposites

From Warrior to Lover - A Journey of Discovery through Norse Mythology

Tim Nilsen

CONTENTS

FOREWORD

In the snowy fjords of Scandinavia, where myth and history interweave like the fine threads of an elaborate tapestry, we encounter one of the most fascinating figures in Norse mythology: Freya. She is more than just another deity in the rich pantheon of Norse gods - she embodies a complex synthesis of power, femininity and spiritual significance that has lost none of its fascination to this day.

When I began to study Norse mythology more intensively, I quickly realized that Freya is a key figure whose significance goes far beyond the usual categorizations. She unites apparent opposites: She is goddess of love and warrior, magician and ruler of life and death, protector and terrifying power. This complexity makes her a timeless figure who can still teach us a lot about the complexity of human existence today.

The history of Freya is deeply rooted in the cultural landscape of Northern Europe. From Sweden to Norway, traces of her worship can be found, testifying to the enormous importance that people once attached to her. But her story is more than just a collection of ancient traditions. It is a window into the minds of our ancestors, their hopes, fears and their understanding of the world.

In this book, I would like to take you on a journey through the various facets of this remarkable goddess. We will trace her possible origins, explore her role in the Norse pantheon and examine the many myths and legends that surround her. We will not only look at the historical sources, but also at the cultural and social contexts in which they arose.

The question of Freya's true origins is particularly fascinating. Was she really, as some researchers assume, originally an aspect of the goddess Frigg that developed into an independent deity over time? Or can we perhaps even trace her roots back to the "Germanic

Isis" mentioned by Tacitus? These questions will guide us through the following chapters.

However, dealing with Freya is not just a look into the past. At a time when we are increasingly searching for orientation and meaning, the old myths can develop new relevance. Freya's various aspects - her connection to nature, her role as protector of home and family, her power over life and death - reflect fundamental human experiences that are still valid today.

This book sees itself as a bridge between the past and the present. It is intended not only to impart knowledge, but also to stimulate reflection on the timeless themes dealt with in the myths surrounding Freya. In doing so, we will take into account both scientific findings and living tradition in order to paint as complete a picture as possible of this fascinating goddess.

Let's delve into the world of Norse mythology together and explore the rich heritage that Freya has left us. Her story is not only a window into the past, but also a mirror in which we can rediscover ourselves and our time.

THE MULTI-FACETED GODDESS

AN INTRODUCTION

In the dazzling world of Norse mythology, Freya stands out as one of the most fascinating and complex deities. Among the goddesses of Asgard, she occupies a special position that cannot be pigeonholed into a single category. She embodies a remarkable synthesis of different spheres of power and aspects that may seem contradictory at first glance, but which come together to form a coherent whole.

North Germanic tradition paints a picture of a goddess of extraordinary versatility. As a member of the vanir, the ancient fertility gods, she brings their original closeness to nature and life-giving power to the company of the Aesir. This combination of different divine traditions makes her a unique figure in the Norse pantheon.

The complexity of Freya is particularly reflected in the various traditions. In the older sources, she appears as a powerful, independent goddess whose influence extends far beyond the usual boundaries of female deities. The Edda poetry paints a particularly complex picture: Here we encounter her as a proud warrior who confidently takes her place among the Aesir, while at the same time retaining her original connection to nature and the elemental forces.

The regional traditions of Scandinavia show different emphases in her worship. While in Norway she was particularly worshipped as the patron goddess of seafaring and the weather, in Sweden her role as a fertility goddess was paramount. These regional variations show the remarkable adaptability of her cult to local needs and traditions.

First and foremost is her role as the goddess of love - not just romantic love, but all facets of this powerful emotion. This responsibility goes far beyond simple matters of love. Freya manifests the transformative power of love, which can both create and destroy. Her connection to beauty is more than superficial; she represents beauty as an expression of divine perfection.

Alongside her role as goddess of love, Freya also reveals a darker, more mysterious side. As a master of Seidr magic, she has powers that go far beyond the mundane. This form of magic, which according to tradition even Odin himself taught her, gives her a special authority in the realm of the supernatural. Seidr magic enables her to see into the future, influence fate and possibly even manipulate life and death.

Particularly noteworthy is her position as goddess of the dead, which puts her in direct competition with Odin. Half of the fallen warriors who come to Valhalla are chosen by her and led to her hall Sessrumnir. This connection to death is only seemingly at odds with her role as the goddess of love and life. Rather, it reveals a deep understanding of the eternal cycle of life and death.

The connection between life and death that manifests itself in Freya goes beyond the usual notion of opposites. Rather, it reveals a deep understanding of the intertwining of these apparent extremes. As a goddess who rules over both the battlefield and the fruits of the earth, she embodies the eternal cycle of becoming and passing away. This synthesis is also reflected in the magical practices attributed to her, where life-giving and life-taking powers are closely interwoven.

Her role as a mediator between different worlds and planes of being is also remarkable. Her ability to transform herself into different forms and travel between worlds makes her an important mediator between the different realms of Norse cosmology. This mobility between the worlds is also reflected in her social role: as a vane goddess in Asgard, she mediates between the various divine spheres of power and contributes to the balance of the cosmic structure.

As the owner of precious magical artifacts such as the Brisingamen necklace and the falcon robe, Freya possesses special means of power. These items are not just jewelry or tools, but symbols of her divine power and authority. They emphasize her position as one of the most powerful goddesses in the Norse pantheon.

Freya's companion animals - her cats and the wild boar Hildesvini - reflect different aspects of her nature. The cats stand for independence, grace and possibly also for the mysterious side of the goddess, while the wild boar symbolizes her connection to wild nature and fertility.

However, Freya's significance goes beyond her mythological functions. The numerous place names in Scandinavia that refer to her bear witness to her widespread veneration. As the patron goddess of house and home, she was possibly also worshipped in private domestic altars, which underlines her importance in people's daily lives.

The complexity of Freya is reflected not least in her various names and manifestations. Each of her names - be it Mardöl, Hörn, Gefn, Syr or Vanades - illuminates a different aspect of her complex nature. This diversity of names points to a goddess whose essence is too rich to be captured in a single name.

In the following chapters, we will examine each of these aspects in more detail and explore the various sources that give us insights into the nature of this fascinating goddess. In doing so, it will become clear that Freya is more than the sum of her various roles - she is an embodiment of the complex and often contradictory nature of divine power itself.

ORIGIN AND ETYMOLOGY

THE MEANING OF HER NAME

Researching the name "Freya" opens a window into the world of thought of the Germanic peoples and their way of understanding the divine. The name itself goes back to the Proto-Germanic root *frawjō, which can be translated as "mistress" or "the first". She shares this basic etymological meaning with her brother Freyr, whose name is the male equivalent.

The linguistic history of the name reflects fundamental social structures. In Old High German, the word "frouwa", the precursor of the modern German word "Frau", developed from the same root. This linguistic development illustrates the central importance of the goddess as the archetype of the feminine in Germanic culture.

The etymological analysis shows further interesting connections to other Germanic languages and dialects. The form "frua" is found in Old Saxon, "frowe" in Old Frisian and "frauja" in Gothic (in the masculine form). These linguistic variants show not only the wide distribution of the name, but also its deep roots in the Germanic language area. Particularly interesting is the development in the various North Germanic dialects, where local peculiarities in pronunciation and spelling developed, which still live on today in regional variants of the name.

The etymological analysis also reveals fascinating connections to other Indo-European languages. Related word stems can be found in Sanskrit, for example, where "priya" means "the beloved". These linguistic parallels possibly point to an even older common root in Indo-European prehistory.

The religious dimension of the name is also evident in various ritual texts and spells that have survived in medieval manuscripts. Here, the name Freya is often mentioned in connection with magical formulas and incantations, which underlines its special power and significance in a religious context. The use of her name in such texts indicates that it was ascribed a magical power of its own.

In the Old Norse sources, Freya's name is often associated with meaningful titles and honorifics. The name "Vanadis", for example, identifies her as the "divine woman of the vanir" and emphasizes her affiliation to this ancient race of gods. This combination of name and title shows how closely her identity is interwoven with her divine origins.

The linguistic analysis also reveals interesting parallels to other European goddesses. Similar connections between divine power and terms of worship can be found in the Roman Venus (related to "venerare" - to worship) or the Greek Aphrodite. These parallels point to similar cultural concepts in various Indo-European societies.

During the Migration Period, when Germanic tribes spread across Europe, different regional variations of the name developed. These variations point to different local cults and interpretations of their divinity. It is possible that the name was originally a title that only later became a proper name -- a development that is frequently observed in religious history.

The use of the name in geographical designations has survived to the present day. In Scandinavian countries, place names can still be found today that refer to former Freya sanctuaries or cult sites. This toponymic evidence proves that the goddess is deeply rooted in the Nordic cultural landscape.

The historical analysis of the name Freya thus reveals a complex linguistic symbol that combines aspects of power, femininity and divine authority. It is a linguistic testimony to the central role that this goddess played in the religious and cultural life of the Germanic peoples and her significance as the embodiment of female power and dignity.

FREYA AND THE VANIR - DIVINE ORIGIN

The story of Freya's origins takes us deep into the mythology of the Norse gods, where she was born as the daughter of the sea god Njord. Her roots with the vanir, a distinct group of gods, fundamentally shape her nature and her later role in Asgard.

The Vanir represent an original layer of the Germanic world of gods. As gods of the elemental forces of nature, they differ fundamentally from the Aesir, who embody order, law and social structures. This fundamental distinction is essential for understanding the later developments in Norse mythology.

The nature of the vanir as fertility gods is particularly evident in their deep connection to the cyclical processes of nature. Archaeological finds from the Migration Period indicate that their worship was closely linked to the agricultural calendar year. Special offerings at spring and autumn festivals, often in the form of precious jewelry or animal sacrifices, testify to the importance of the vanir for the prosperity of crops and the fertility of livestock. The wans were not just seen as passive recipients of offerings, but as active participants in the prosperity of the community.

The social structure of the vanir differed significantly from that of the Aesir. While the Aesir represented a strictly hierarchical, war-oriented society, there is much to suggest that the vanir embodied a more egalitarian form of society. The practice of sibling marriage among the vanir mentioned in the sources could be an indication of other kinship concepts and social structures. These different social models also shaped the later development of Norse religion, in which both concepts coexisted.

The magical practices of the vanir were of a special kind and differed from the magic of the Aesir. While the Aesir were more associated with direct, often warlike magic, the magic of the vanir was more subtle and more connected to the forces of nature. This form of magic, which later became known as Seidr, included practices such as divination, healing and influencing the weather. Freya's transmission of these magical arts to the Aesir marks an important moment of cultural exchange between the two deities.

Freya's father Njord, the god of the seas and seafaring, fathered her with his sister - a detail that illustrates the fundamentally different moral concepts of the vanir. Among the vanir, unions between siblings were not uncommon, which also explains the early relationship between Freya and her brother Freyr. This practice was only forbidden when she was admitted to Asgard.

The anonymity of Freya's mother in the traditions leaves room for speculation. This could point to lost traditions or to the fact that the mother figure was deliberately omitted in later, Christian-influenced traditions.

The geographical home of the vanir is described in the sources as Vanaheim, a realm that is clearly distinct from Asgard. Vanaheim is described as a fertile, water-rich land, reflecting the nature of the vanir as fertility gods. However, the exact nature of this realm remains largely obscure in the lore.

The vanir are described in the lore as extraordinarily wealthy and blessed with magical powers. This association with wealth and supernatural abilities is reflected in Freya's later character, particularly in her association with precious jewelry and her mastery of Seidr magic. The material wealth of the vanir is symbolic of the abundance and fertility of nature.

As a vane goddess, Freya brought certain characteristic traits with her to Asgard: her deep connection to nature, her magical abilities and her freer conception of love and sexuality. These attributes clearly distinguish her from the Aesir goddesses and remain even after her integration into the society of the Aesir.

Freya's origins are also reflected in her special relationship with the forces of nature. Her ability to take the form of a falcon, her connection to cats and her relationship with the wild boar Hildesvingi underline the deep connection to nature that is characteristic of the vanir.

The fact that Freya became one of the most important goddesses in Asgard despite her vanir origins testifies to her special position and importance. She embodies a successful synthesis between the original natural forces of the vanir and the orderly society of the Aesir, which makes her a unique figure in the Norse pantheon.

The cultural significance of the vanir is reflected in various archaeological finds. Cult sites and offerings associated with the worship of the wans often show a close connection to fertility rites and nature worship. This material evidence supports the literary sources in their depiction of the vanir as gods of natural vitality.

The finds of ritual objects and cult images associated with vanir worship are particularly revealing. Miniature golden figurines, possibly depicting Freya or other vanir deities, have been found in various places in Scandinavia. These artifacts often show a combination of symbols of fertility and magical power, emphasizing the dual nature of the vanir deities.

The relationship between the vanir and humans seems to have been more direct and personal than that of the Aesir. While the Aesir are often portrayed as distant, majestic deities, the vanir appear in the traditions as closer to the daily lives of humans. This closeness is also reflected in the sacrificial customs, which were less formal and hierarchical than the rituals of Aesir worship.

Mythological lore also points to a special connection between the vanir and time and fate. Unlike the Aesir, who often fight against fate, the vanir seem to have a deeper understanding of natural cycles and the inevitability of change. This wisdom, which Freya brings with her to Asgard, contributes to her reputation as a seer and diviner.

Freya's vanir origins also explain her special role in rites of passage and transformation processes. As a goddess who has herself made the transition from one family of gods to another, she becomes the patroness of all transitions in life. This function is particularly evident in her significance at weddings, initiation rites and funerals.

THE VANIR WAR AND GULLVEIG

The Wan War represents one of the most significant conflicts in Norse mythology -- a war between the two deities that fundamentally changed not only the fate of Freya, but the entire divine order. At the center of this conflict is a mysterious figure named Gullveig, whose possible connection to Freya is one of the most interesting mysteries of Norse mythology.

The events that led to the Wan War begin with the arrival of Gullveig among the Aesir. Her name, which can be translated as "gold rush" or "gold power", already indicates a close connection to gold and wealth -- attributes that are also attributed to Freya. According to tradition, Gullveig came to the Aesir and practiced a form of magic that awakened in them a lust for gold and wealth.

The historical context of the Vane War is of particular interest to researchers. Some scholars see reflections of real historical conflicts between different cult groups in the early Germanic period in the mythological narrative. The differences between the Aesir and vanir could therefore represent different religious and social systems that clashed during the Migration Period. The connection to gold and wealth could indicate the increasing importance of trade routes and economic influence during this period.

The Aesir's reaction to Gullveig was extreme: they tried to burn her three times in Odin's hall. But each time she rose again from the ashes, underlining her supernatural nature. After the third time, she was given the name Heid ("the shining one" or "the radiant one") and became a powerful seer who practiced Seidr magic -- a form of magic that is later clearly associated with Freya.

The burning of Gullveig three times has a deep symbolic meaning. The number three often appears in Norse mythology as a symbol of transformation and completion. The attempt to destroy Gullveig by fire could be interpreted as a failed attempt at purification. Instead, the burning leads to an increase in her power - a motif reminiscent of initiation rites and shamanistic transformation processes. The change of name from Gullveig to Heid marks the completion of this transformation.

The parallels between Gullveig and Freya are remarkable: both are associated with gold and wealth, both are masters of Seidr magic, and both have a transformative nature. The thesis that Gullveig could possibly be another name or manifestation of Freya is supported by these similarities. However, there is no clear confirmation of this connection in the sources.

The attempt to kill Gullveig led to the outbreak of the vanir War. The vanir saw the treatment of Gullveig as an unacceptable affront. The ensuing war is described in the sources as fierce and costly. The vanir proved to be equal opponents to the Aesir, which underlines their great power. Their magical abilities in particular made them dangerous opponents.

The strategic aspects of the vanir war are presented differently in various sources. Some traditions emphasize the superior fighting power of the Aesir, while others focus on the magical abilities of the vanir. Of particular interest is the mention of special magical warfare by the vanir, which possibly points to ancient practices of ritual warfare. The use of weather magic and other supernatural powers shows that this conflict was fought on several levels.

The first act of war in this conflict was highly symbolic: Odin threw his spear over the enemy army - a gesture that traditionally initiated a war. The vanir countered with powerful magic and even managed to break through the walls of Asgard. This episode clearly shows the conflict between physical strength (Aesir) and magical power (vanir).

The war finally ended with a peace treaty, which was sealed by an exchange of hostages. Njord and his children Freya and Freyr went to Asgard as hostages, while the Aesir sent Hönir and Mimir to the vanir. This exchange was intended to secure peace between the gods and ultimately led to the integration of the vanir into the society of the Aesir.

Freya's role in this conflict remains largely obscure. If she is indeed identical to Gullveig, she would have been both the trigger and part of the peace solution to the war. This dual role would emphasize her complex nature as a figure of transition and transformation.

The cultural effects of the peace treaty were far-reaching. The exchange of hostages led not only to a political, but also to a cultural mixing of the two deities. The integration of the vanir into the society of the Aesir brought with it new religious practices and ideas. The influence of Seidr magic in particular on Norse society can be traced back to this fusion.

The consequences of the vanir War were far-reaching. The integration of the vanir into Asgard led to a synthesis of the various divine powers. Freya established herself as a powerful goddess in Asgard and brought Seidr magic to the Aesir. Even Odin learned this form of magic from her, which underlines the importance of the cultural exchange between the gods.

The story of Gullveig and the Wan War also sheds an interesting light on the role of gold and wealth in Norse mythology. The destructive power of the lust for gold awakened by Gullveig contrasts with Freya's positive connection to gold and treasure. Perhaps this ambivalence is the key to understanding the complex relationship between Gullveig and Freya.

The archaeological findings from the Migration Period provide remarkable support for the mythological tradition of the vanir War. Numerous weapon sacrifices and ritual depositions of war booty in the bogs and lakes of Scandinavia point to intense military conflicts, which may also have had religious dimensions. The connection between warfare and religious rituals, as described in the vanir War, can also be found in this archaeological evidence.

The significance of the exchange of hostages for the later development of the Norse religion is particularly revealing. This practice, which is also well documented in historical sources, served not only to secure peace, but also to promote cultural exchange. The hostages were often high-ranking personalities who acted as cultural mediators in their new environment. Freya's role as a hostage in Asgard could therefore also be seen as a model for the integration of different religious traditions.

The vanir War and its consequences are an example of the complexity of religious developments in the Germanic world. The fusion of different cults and traditions, which is reflected in the mythological narrative, was probably a lengthy process that extended over centuries. The story of Gullveig and the Wan War possibly preserves the memory of these fundamental cultural transformations.

The repercussions of the Viking War extended into the Viking Age. The synthesis of Aesir and Vane cults, which is reflected in mythology, was reflected in the religious practices of the Norse peoples. The worship of deities of both sexes and the integration of various magical traditions shaped Norse religion until it was replaced by Christianity.

THE POWER OF MAGIC – FREYA AND SEIDR

Seidr magic is one of the most complex and fascinating forms of Nordic magic. As a magical tradition in its own right, it differs fundamentally from other magical practices such as rune magic. The Ynglinga saga tells us that this art originally came from the vanir and was brought to the Aesir by Freya.

The historical sources describe Seidr as a multi-faceted magical practice that encompassed various areas: divination (the art of divination), weather manipulation, healing and also damaging spells. In contrast to rune magic, which was strongly associated with Odin and often practiced by males, Seidr was traditionally a female domain. This gender assignment was also reflected in the social structure of the North Germanic peoples, where female seers played an important social and religious role.

The connection between Seidr and the shamanistic practices of other northern Eurasian peoples is particularly remarkable. The technique of ritual singing, which played a central role in Seidr, shows striking parallels to shamanistic singing traditions. The so-called "vardlokkur" or "spirit lure chant" was used to put the seer into a trance and summon spirits or other supernatural beings. These chants were often performed by a choir of supporting women, which indicates the communal nature of important Seidr rituals.

The practice of Seidr followed specific ritual patterns. Central to this was the elevated Seidr seat from which the seer practiced their art. Archaeological finds have confirmed the existence of such ritual structures. The ceremonies often included ecstatic elements, which were evoked by singing and special movements. This aspect clearly distinguished Seidr from other magical practices in the Nordic world.

The ethical implications of Seidr were complex. While the art could be used for positive purposes such as healing and divination, it was also used for harmful magic. This duality is reflected in various sagas, where Seidr practitioners appear as both wise counselors and feared sorcerers. The power of Seidr was both respected and feared.

Archaeological findings have considerably expanded our understanding of Seidr practice in recent decades. Grave finds with special ritual objects, such as certain staffs and amulets, provide insights into the material culture of this magical tradition. Particularly revealing are the so-called "Völva graves", burials of presumed seeresses, which were often richly decorated with symbolic grave goods. These finds indicate the high social status of the Seidr practitioners.

The transmission of the Seidr art followed strict traditional patterns. The knowledge was usually passed on from teacher to pupil, and the training could take years. This tradition of passing on magical knowledge can be found in various Nordic sagas, which tell of powerful seers who passed on their knowledge to selected students.

The ritual tools and symbols of Seidr were of great importance. Staffs, special robes and amulets played an important role in the practice. Archaeological finds of such objects in the graves of presumed Seidr practitioners give us an insight into the material culture of this magical tradition.

The connection between Seidr and the forces of nature played a special role. The ability to influence the weather or communicate with animals was considered an essential part of this magic. The Seidr practitioner had to develop a deep understanding of natural cycles and the connections between different forces of nature. This close connection to nature distinguished Seidr from other, more formalized magical traditions.

The connection between Seidr and ideas of fate was of particular importance. The ability to see into the future and influence fate was a central aspect of this magic. This linked Seidr with fundamental concepts of the Norse worldview, such as the concept of fate of the Wyrd and the idea of the Norns as weavers of fate.

The practice of divination in the Seidr differed significantly from other forms of divination. While rune casting, for example, was based on clear symbols and their interpretation, the Seidr worked with visionary experiences and direct spiritual communication. The seer received her visions in a state of trance, acting as an intermediary between the material world and the supernatural realms. This form of divination was particularly consulted when making important communal decisions.

The connection between Seidr and the forces of nature was particularly strong. As a form of magic originating from the vanir, Seidr was closely connected to the cycles of nature and the elemental forces. This connection to nature was evident in his ability to influence the weather, communicate with animals and use medicinal herbs.

The transformation of Seidr after Christianization is a fascinating chapter in religious history. Elements of this magical tradition survived in folk customs and healing arts, often in a Christianized or secularized form. The continuity of certain magical practices shows the deep roots of Seidr in Nordic culture.

In recent decades, scientific research into Seidr has provided new insights into the complexity of this magical tradition. Archaeological finds, literary sources and religious analyses now enable a more differentiated understanding of this fascinating form of Nordic magic.

The social dimension of Seidr in Nordic society is particularly interesting. The Seidr practitioner often occupied a special position that placed her outside the normal social hierarchies. This position enabled her to act as an independent advisor and mediator. At the same time, this special role also brought with it social isolation and sometimes stigmatization, especially when the Seidr was used for harmful purposes.

FREYA AND LOVE – ASPECTS OF A GODDESS OF LOVE

Of all the Norse deities, Freya is the one most closely associated with love in all its facets. Her role as goddess of love goes far beyond that of a simple patron of romantic relationships - she embodies the transformative power of love in all its manifestations.

Love magic was an important aspect of Freya's work. According to tradition, it was particularly useful to invoke her in matters of love. This form of magic differed from other magical practices due to its direct connection to the emotional and physical aspects of love. Special rituals and invocations were specifically dedicated to Freya and were used to find a partner, strengthen existing relationships and heal heartache.

Archaeological finds prove the importance of love rituals in the Freya cult. Amulets and offerings clearly associated with love magic have been found at various cult sites. Of particular interest are small figurines and pieces of jewelry that were worn as personal talismans. Analysis of these artifacts reveals a complex symbolic language that combines aspects of love, fertility and divine power.

Unlike the Greek Aphrodite, for example, Freya is not exclusively associated with physical beauty and desire. Her connection to love also encompasses deeper aspects such as fidelity, longing and the transformative power of love, which is particularly evident in her own story with Odr. This multi-layered view of love reflects a complex understanding of human relationships.

As the goddess of love, Freya was particularly revered by women. In Nordic societies, she played an important role in weddings and other rites of passage related to love and partnership. Archaeological finds of amulets and other cult objects bear witness to this intense worship.

The ritual practices associated with Freya's love aspect were varied and complex. Traditions tell of nocturnal ceremonies in which young women asked for Freya's assistance in choosing a partner. Such rituals often took place at certain places of power, such as sacred groves or springs, which were associated with the goddess. The timing of these rituals was often based on the phases of the moon and seasonal festivals, which underlines the close connection between love magic and natural cycles.

The connection between love and beauty finds a special expression in Freya. Her beauty is not portrayed as superficial, but as an expression of her divine nature. The famous Brisingamen necklace symbolizes this connection between beauty, love and divine power.

Freya's view of love is also reflected in her self-determined approach to relationships. The myths tell of how she resolutely rejects advances from giants and makes her own decisions in matters of love. This autonomy makes her a role model of female self-determination.

Another interesting aspect is the connection between love and war in Freya's character. As the ruler of half of the fallen warriors, she unites apparent opposites. This connection shows that love in Norse mythology was not understood as weak or passive, but as a force that can be just as powerful as martial strength.

The significance of the goddess of love Freya thus goes far beyond romantic notions. She embodies a complex understanding of love that combines personal relationships, social order and cosmic forces. In her person, the transformative power of love is revealed as a fundamental principle of the Nordic worldview.

The literary sources show a remarkable differentiation in the depiction of Freya's love aspects. In the Edda songs, she often appears as a self-confident goddess who affirms her sexuality, while the sagas tend to emphasize her role as a protector of marriage and family. These different facets of her nature possibly reflect different social ideas and regional traditions.

Freya's understanding of love also encompasses its creative power. As the goddess of fertility, she combines the personal, emotional dimension of love with its life-giving power. This holistic view of love sets her apart from the more one-dimensional love goddesses of other mythologies.

The traditional love rituals in honor of Freya are remarkably complex. They included not only requests for romantic fulfillment, but also rituals for personal development and spiritual transformation. These practices reflect an understanding of love that goes far beyond the romantic.

The connection between love magic and the seasonal festivals is particularly revealing. The most important rituals often took place during the spring and summer festivals, when the awakening nature symbolized the life-giving power of the goddess. This temporal integration of love rituals into the natural cycle of the year underlines the close connection between love, fertility and cosmic order in the Nordic world view.

The archaeological finds of love amulets and ritual objects provide further insights into the practical practice of Freya worship. Many of these objects combine symbols of love with protective signs, indicating that Freya was invoked not only as the goddess of love, but also as the protector of lovers. The careful design of these amulets shows the great importance attached to the material manifestation of divine powers.

THE GOLDEN TEARS - FREYA AND ODR

The relationship between Freya and the mysterious god Odr is one of the most poetic and at the same time most enigmatic stories in Norse mythology. This connection, characterized by longing and eternal searching, reveals a surprisingly vulnerable side of the powerful goddess and led to one of the most beautiful metaphors in Norse poetry: Freya's golden tears.

The sources for the story of Freya and Odr are varied, but often contradictory. While some traditions tell of a happy beginning for the couple, other texts suggest that their relationship was characterized by Odr's restlessness from the very beginning. These different versions could indicate different regional traditions or different chronological layers of myth formation. The complexity of the tradition reflects the complexity of the relationship itself.

After her arrival in Asgard, Freya chose the ace Odr as her companion. Surprisingly little is known about Odr himself - he appears in the lore almost exclusively in connection with Freya. This scarcity of sources has led to various speculations about his true identity. Some researchers have suggested that Odr may be a manifestation of Odin due to the similarity of his name. However, this thesis is refuted by various sources, which clearly present Odr as an independent figure.

The marriage between Freya and Odr produced two daughters: Hnoss and Gersemi, both of whose names mean "jewel" or "treasure". This naming emphasizes the connection between Freya and precious things, which runs through many aspects of her nature. The daughters are described as embodiments of their mother's beauty and wealth.

The names of the daughters have a deeper symbolic meaning. In skaldic poetry, the terms "Hnoss" and "Gersemi" are often used as kenningar (poetic paraphrases) for particularly valuable things. This linguistic connection between Freya's offspring and the concept of value reinforces the idea of the goddess as the source of all wealth. The daughters can also be understood as manifestations of the creative power of love.

The central element in the story of Freya and Odr is his frequent absence. Odr is described as a restless wanderer who often goes on long journeys. During these journeys, Freya uses her magical abilities to search for him. In her longing, she roams the various worlds, often in the form of a falcon. This search has a deeply symbolic character and is reminiscent of similar myths in other cultures.

Mythological research sees various possible levels of meaning in Odr and Freya's quest. One interpretation sees the story as an allegory for the changing of the seasons, with Odr's absence symbolizing winter. Other interpretations see it as a metaphor for the spiritual quest or the transformative power of longing. The various possible interpretations show the complexity of the myth.

Freya's travels in search of Odr show a special application of her magical powers. Unlike ritual or divinatory practices, here she uses her magic for deeply personal reasons. The transformation into a falcon, the adoption of different names and forms - all this serves the goal of finding her beloved Odr again.

The transformational aspects of the quest are particularly revealing. The ability to take on different forms is understood in the sources not only as a magical technique, but also as an expression of emotional transformation. Each new form that Freya takes on reflects a different aspect of her longing. The falcon form particularly symbolizes the freedom and expansiveness of her quest.

The golden tears that Freya sheds during her quest became an important element of scaldic poetry. The idea that her tears turn to gold shows the transformative power of her emotions. Gold is often described in Norse poetry as "Freya's tears" - a poetic metaphor that combines beauty and pain.

The story of Freya and Odr also shows an interesting reversal of traditional gender roles. While in many myths the male hero goes off on an adventure and the woman stays behind, here it is the goddess who actively searches for her lover. This activity and initiative suits Freya's self-determined character.

The emotional complexity of the relationship between Freya and Odr is particularly evident in the various accounts of their encounters. Some sources tell of brief, intense reunions, but these are always followed by renewed partings. This cyclical nature of their relationship reinforces the mythological nature of the story and links it to universal themes of loss and reunion.

It is also remarkable how the search for Odr Freyas combines different aspects. As a lover she shows deep emotions, as a magician she uses her supernatural powers, and as a wanderer between the worlds she demonstrates her cosmological significance. The story thus combines personal feelings with divine power.

The archaeological finds complement the literary picture of the Freya-Odr story. Votive offerings were found at various cult sites, which may be connected to the invocation of Freya in times of need. Golden tear beads and falcon amulets in particular could be interpreted as material evidence of these aspects of the Freya cult. These finds indicate that the story of Freya and Odr was not only told as a myth, but was also ritually reenacted.

Freya's fidelity to Odr stands in interesting contrast to her other reputation as a free love goddess. While she is often associated with various loves, her relentless pursuit of Odr shows a deep emotional attachment and constancy in love. This apparent contradiction underlines the complexity of her nature.

The eternal search for the absent lover also has cosmological significance. Some interpretations see Odr's journeys and Freya's search for him as a metaphor for the changing of the seasons or other cyclical natural processes. This would fit in with Freya's origins as a wan goddess and her connection to the forces of nature.

The myth of Freya and Odr also has parallels in other Indo-European traditions. Similar stories of searching goddesses can be found in the myth of Isis and Osiris or in the story of Demeter and Persephone. These parallels point to a common mythological motif that thematizes the connection between love, loss and cosmic order.

BRISINGAMEN - THE MOST PRECIOUS PIECE OF JEWELRY

The Brisingamen, often referred to as the most beautiful piece of jewelry in the world, is far more than a precious necklace - it is a central symbol of divine power and a key to understanding Freya's nature. The story of its creation and the myths associated with it reveal important aspects of her personality and her position in the divine hierarchy.

The name "Brisingamen" is not only a name, but also carries a deep mythological meaning. The linguistic analysis of the name opens up various possible interpretations. The connection to the Old Norse word for "fire" (brísingr) could point to the transformative power of the piece of jewelry. Other interpretations see a connection to the Brisingar dwarves, whose craftsmanship created the necklace. These various etymologies reflect the complexity of the mythological symbol.

A detailed description of the Brisingamen can be found in various sources. It is described as a necklace of extraordinary beauty, often set with shining gemstones and of such radiance that it could illuminate the darkness. The material properties of the piece of jewelry are always understood as an expression of its supernatural powers. Of particular interest are references to its ability to transform or protect the wearer.

The name "Brisingamen" itself is the subject of scientific debate. One possible interpretation derives the name from the Old Norse "brísingr" (fire), which could refer to the sparkling, fiery shine of the piece of jewelry. Other theories link the name to the "Brisingar", the dwarves who created the necklace.

There are several versions of the story of how the Brisingamen came to be. The best known tells how Freya discovered four dwarf smiths at work. These dwarves, the Brisingar, had created a necklace of incomparable beauty. Freya, overwhelmed by the sight of it, offered the dwarves gold and silver in exchange.

The craftsmanship of the dwarves is particularly emphasized in the sources. As inhabitants of the subterranean realms and masters of metalworking, they possessed secret knowledge and magical abilities. The Brisingamen is described as the pinnacle of their art, combining technical perfection with supernatural power. The descriptions of the manufacturing process indicate complex metallurgical and magical techniques that made the jewelry more than a mere ornament.

However, the dwarves set an unusual condition: they would only give her the collar if she spent one night with each of them. This condition and Freya's decision to accept it have led to various interpretations. Some see it as a reference to ancient fertility rites, others interpret it as a metaphor for the price that beauty and power can exact.

An important story about the Brisingamen revolves around its theft by Loki. The cunning god sneaked into Freya's chambers and stole the necklace. The theft was noticed by Heimdall, who then became embroiled in a dramatic battle with Loki. This battle, which according to tradition took place on a rock on the coast, ended with Heimdall's victory and the return of the necklace to Freya.

The episode of the theft is described differently in various sources. Some versions report that Loki transformed himself into a fly to enter Freya's chamber, while others speak of his ability to make himself invisible. The battle between Heimdall and Loki is described as a duel in which both gods took the form of seals - a detail that emphasizes the connection to transformation magic and the forces of nature.

The symbolic meaning of the Brisingamen goes far beyond its material value. As a jewel of the goddess of love and fertility, it represents the connection between beauty, desire and power. Its creation by dwarves, who in Norse mythology are regarded as masters of transforming raw materials into precious objects, underlines this symbolic dimension.

The magical properties of the necklace are described differently in various traditions. Some sources speak of its ability to give the wearer supernatural beauty or special magical powers. Other texts suggest that the Brisingamen played a role in Freya's transformations, especially her ability to take on the form of a falcon. The connection between the piece of jewelry and Freya's magical abilities is portrayed as inseparable.

The parallel to other mythological jewelry is interesting. Like Freya's Brisingamen, there are also powerful necklaces and jewelry in other mythologies that are often associated with female deities. This points to a deeper symbolic meaning of such jewelry as a sign of divine power.

The loss and recovery of the Brisingamen can also be interpreted as a metaphor for the cyclical nature of nature. Just as the seasons change and nature dies and reawakens, the necklace is also lost and found again. This interpretation would fit Freya's role as a fertility goddess.

The Brisingamen also plays an important role in later lore. It is described as a source of special magical powers that give Freya additional abilities. This idea of jewelry as a carrier of magical power can also be found in other mythological and folkloristic traditions.

The connection between the Brisingamen and pre-Christian cult practices is of particular interest to religious history. Archaeological finds of precious necklaces in ritual contexts indicate that such jewelry played an important role in religious ceremonies. The mythological significance of the Brisingamen could therefore also reflect real cult practices.

The story of the Brisingamen shows the complex relationship between the various divine and mythological beings. Dwarves as creators, Loki as thief, Heimdall as protector - all play their part in the network of relationships and conflicts that characterize Norse mythology.

The Brisingamen also occupies a special place in skaldic poetry. It is often used as a metaphor for supreme beauty and divine power. The poetic descriptions of the necklace emphasize both its material splendour and its supernatural significance.

ATTRIBUTES AND COMPANIONS - CATS, FALCON ROBE AND HILDESVINI

Freya's special attributes and companion animals are not only symbols of her divine power, but also reveal central aspects of her nature. Each of these attributes carries its own symbolic meaning and refers to different facets of her divine nature.

Freya's connection to her cats goes back deep into Germanic mythology. The two large gray cats pulling her chariot are described differently in various sources. Some traditions speak of wild forest cats, others of mysterious creatures that were larger than ordinary domestic cats. Like Freya herself, these companion animals combine seemingly contradictory characteristics - they are simultaneously tame and wild, graceful and dangerous, domesticated and independent.

The mythological significance of cats is confirmed by archaeological finds. Cat representations and bones have been found in various Scandinavian graves, especially those associated with the cult of Freya. These finds indicate that cats played an important role not only in mythology but also in practical worship. Particularly interesting are amulets in the shape of cats, which may have been used as protective symbols or to invoke Freya.

The connection between Freya and cats goes beyond their role as draught animals. As sleek, nocturnal predators, they embody many of the qualities that are also associated with Freya: Independence, grace, but also a certain dangerousness. These qualities reflect different aspects of Freya's own nature and emphasize her complex nature as a goddess.

The special relationship between the goddess and her cats is also reflected in various ritual practices. Some traditions report that cats had to be present during certain magical rituals. It was believed that they could act as intermediaries between the human and divine spheres. This idea led to cats being regarded not only as farm animals but also as sacred animals in many Nordic households.

The falcon robe or falcon dress (fjaðrhamr) is another central attribute of Freya. This magical garment enables her to transform into a falcon and fly through the air. The ability to transform is an important aspect of Freya's magical power and demonstrates her ability to transcend the limitations of physical form.

The symbolism of the falcon is multi-layered: as a bird of prey, it embodies power and freedom, while at the same time it stands for keen powers of observation and foresight. The connection to the falcon underlines Freya's role as a goddess who can switch between different worlds and forms of being. This mobility between spheres is a central aspect of her divine power.

The falcon robe appears in several important myths. Freya occasionally lends it to other gods for important missions - Loki in particular uses it several times. These loans show Freya's willingness to cooperate, even if her relationships with the other gods are not always free of tension.

The falcon as a transformational figure has a special mythological significance. In contrast to other forms of transformation, which are often associated with cunning or deception, the falcon shape represents a higher form of transformation. It not only enables physical movement through the air, but also symbolizes the ability for spiritual elevation and an overview of the different worlds.

Another important companion is the wild boar Hildesvini, whose name can be translated as "fighting boar". She shares this connection to the wild boar with her brother Freyr, who also has a boar as a companion. In Germanic culture, wild boars were regarded as powerful symbols of strength and fertility.

Archaeological finds confirm the importance of the boar in the Nordic cult. Numerous depictions of boars, often in the form of jewelry or ritual objects, have been found in graves and at cult sites. Of particular interest are the so-called "boar helmets", which were worn by warriors and may represent a link between the warlike and cultic aspects of the boar.

Hildesvini is described in the sources as an exceptionally large and strong animal whose golden bristles glow in the dark. These glowing bristles possibly symbolize a connection to solar aspects or to the transformative power of fire. The mythological significance of the boar goes far beyond its physical appearance. As an animal associated with both fertility and martial power, it reflects the duality in Freya's own being.

The combination of these different companion animals - cats, falcon and wild boar - reflects the different aspects of Freya's nature. She combines the grace of the cats, the freedom of the falcon and the wild power of the wild boar. This combination emphasizes her role as a goddess who unites different, seemingly contradictory aspects.

Companion animals also have a cosmological dimension. In many myths, they act as mediators between different worlds or states of being. The cats pull Freya's chariot through the air, the falcon enables travel between worlds, and the wild boar connects her to the forces of the earth. These different levels of movement and connection make Freya a truly cosmic goddess.

FOLKWANG AND SESSRUMNIR

FREYA'S EMPIRE

In Asgard, the home of the gods, Freya has her own realm: the place Folkwang with the magnificent hall Sessrumnir. These places are not only the residence of the goddess, but also have deep symbolic and mythological significance, especially in relation to Freya's role as goddess of the dead.

Folkwang, whose name can be translated as "field of the people" or "field of the army", is an important place in the cosmology of Norse mythology. The name already indicates its function: it is a place of communion where the souls of the deceased gather. The interpretation as the "field of the army" refers in particular to Freya's role in receiving fallen warriors.

Archaeological investigations of cult sites associated with Freya reveal interesting parallels with the mythological description of Folkwang. Many of these sites are located on elevated, open areas that allow a wide view over the landscape. This geographical location could reflect the idea of Folkwang as a place between heaven and earth. Finds of weapons and jewelry at these sites indicate their importance as sacrificial sites.

Sessrumnir, Freya's hall, whose name means "the one with many seats" or "hall of many seats", stands in the middle of Folkwang. This name is indicative of its function as a meeting place. Interestingly, Sessrumnir is mentioned in the sources not only as a hall, but also as a ship -- a double meaning that possibly refers to the importance of ships in the Nordic cult of the dead.

The dual nature of Sessrumnir as a hall and a ship has profound symbolic significance. In Norse culture, ships played a central role in both life and death. The famous ship burials of the Viking Age bear witness to the idea that the deceased had to embark on a journey. Sessrumnir combines these two aspects: As a hall, it provides a home for the deceased; as a ship, it enables the journey between worlds.

The architectural description of Sessrumnir in the sources is less detailed than that of Odin's Valhalla. Nevertheless, various indications suggest that it was a place of extraordinary splendor, corresponding to Freya's status as goddess of beauty and wealth. The many seats indicate large festivals and gatherings.

The function of Folkwang and Sessrumnir is particularly significant in connection with the fate of the dead. According to tradition, Freya chooses half of those who die in battle for herself, while the other half goes to Odin in Valhalla. This shows her equal status with Odin in terms of receiving the deceased.

The organization of daily life in Sessrumnir is depicted differently in the sources than the warlike activities in Valhalla. While Odin's Einherjar fight and celebrate daily, the inhabitants of Sessrumnir seem to lead a more varied life. The lore speaks of music, poetry and other artistic activities, which fits in with Freya's role as the goddess of beauty and culture.

The parallel between Sessrumnir and Valhalla is remarkable. Both halls serve as a resting place for fallen warriors, but while Valhalla is often associated with masculine warrior virtues, Sessrumnir seems to represent a different aspect of warrior life. Here, martial aspects are possibly combined with Freya's role as a goddess of love and fertility.

The idea of Sessrumnir as a ship is particularly interesting in the context of Norse burial customs. Ship burials were widespread among the Norse, and the idea of a ship as a transition between the world of the living and the dead can be found in many cultures. Sessrumnir could therefore be understood as a cosmic ship that receives the souls of the deceased.

Another significant aspect is the organization of life in Folkwang. According to tradition, Freya not only gathers the fallen warriors here, but also her servants and retainers. This points to a complex social structure that may represent the idealized image of a Norse court.

According to tradition, the architectural design of Folkwang reflects the nature of the vanir. As an open field, it stands in contrast to the fortified halls of the Aesir and is reminiscent of the original connection of the vanir to the great outdoors. The descriptions emphasize the vastness and fertility of the land, underlining Freya's role as the goddess of fertility.

The design of Folkwang as a "field" could also point to Freya's origins as a vanir goddess. The vanir were closely associated with the fertility of the earth, and a field as the dwelling place of their most powerful representative seems particularly fitting in this context. This would create a link between Freya's different aspects as a goddess of death and fertility.

The significance of Folkwang and Sessrumnir thus goes far beyond their function as the mere dwelling place of a goddess. They are central places in the cosmological structure of Norse mythology, where various aspects of Freya's nature - as goddess of death, as ruler and as vanir goddess - manifest themselves. The dual nature of Sessrumnir as a hall and a ship reflects the complexity and multi-layered nature of Freya herself.

THE GODDESS OF THE DEAD

RULER OVER FALLEN WARRIORS

One of the most fascinating and perhaps surprising aspects of Freya is her role as goddess of the dead. This function, which at first glance seems to contradict her position as the goddess of love and life, reveals a deeper dimension of her nature and the Norse concept of death on closer inspection.

The connection between death and life, which manifests itself in Freya, corresponds to a deeply rooted understanding of Germanic religiosity. In the Norse worldview, death and life were not seen as absolute opposites, but as different aspects of a continuous cycle. Freya's role as goddess of the dead is therefore not an anomaly, but a natural extension of her life-giving power.

The Edda reports that Freya chooses half of the battle dead for herself each day, while the other half goes to Odin. This division of the fallen between Freya and Odin is remarkable as it suggests an equality between the two deities in terms of receiving the dead. It is one of the few situations in which a goddess enjoys the same privileges as the father of the gods himself.

The criteria according to which Freya makes her selection are not explicitly mentioned in the sources. In contrast to Odin's Einherjar, who train in Valhalla for the final battle at Ragnarök, the stay of the fallen in Folkwang seems to serve a different purpose. Some interpretations see a connection here to Freya's aspects as a goddess of love and fertility -- perhaps her chosen warriors represent other qualities than the purely martial ones.

The archaeological findings support this interpretation. In graves associated with the cult of Freya, there are not only weapons but also objects that indicate artistic or craft activities. This could indicate that Freya's entourage consisted not only of warriors in the narrower sense, but also of people who were characterized by other skills.

A particularly revealing reference to Freya's role as goddess of the dead can be found in the saga of Egil Skallagrimsson. When Egil is in deep mourning over the death of his sons and refuses to eat, his daughter Thorgerd declares that she too will not eat until she "dines with Freya". This statement shows that the transition to Freya's realm was not seen as a terrible fate, but as an honorable alternative.

It is also worth noting that Freya's reception of the dead was not limited to male warriors. The aforementioned episode with Thorgerd suggests that women could also be admitted to Freya's hall, which is an interesting contrast to the often male-dominated notion of Valhalla. This could point to older ideas of female warriorship or a broader definition of 'honorable death'.

The ritual practice of worshipping the dead under Freya's aegis reveals interesting peculiarities. Archaeological finds indicate that certain burial rites were specifically associated with her cult. Graves containing both warlike and cultic objects are particularly revealing. The burial of cat or falcon amulets could be understood as a direct reference to Freya as the goddess of the dead.

The connection between death and fertility, which manifests itself in Freya, is a common motif in various cultures. Death is not seen as the final end, but as part of a larger cycle of death and rebirth. Freya's position as a goddess of death and fertility could reflect this cyclical idea.

According to tradition, when Freya goes into battle, she is accompanied by her chosen warriors. This shows that the fallen in her realm do not remain in passive expectation, but actively participate in divine events. This idea differs from that of the training Einherjar in Valhalla and points to a different kind of post-mortal existence.

The archaeological finds support the literary sources with regard to Freya's role in the cult of the dead. Grave goods that can be associated with Freya, such as cat or falcon amulets, point to her importance in the funeral rites. Of particular interest is the discovery of a grave of a presumed priestess in Sweden who wore an amulet of Freya.

The idea of Sessrumnir as a ship gains additional significance in this context. In the Nordic tradition, ships played an important role in the cult of the dead, as evidenced by the famous ship burials. The dual nature of Freya's hall as a building and a ship could therefore also symbolize its function as a place of transition between life and death.

Freya's role as goddess of the dead also shows interesting parallels to other Indo-European goddesses who are associated with both life and death. This combination of apparent opposites -- life and death, love and war -- seems to be a recurring motif in the religious imagination of the Indo-European peoples.

The transformation and integration of death rituals into Christian customs is a fascinating chapter in the history of religion. Many elements of Freya worship in connection with death were adopted into Christian cults of saints or transformed into popular religious practices. The continuity of certain burial customs and death rituals into the Christian era testifies to the deep roots of these ideas in Nordic culture.

In this complex role as goddess of the dead, the complexity of Freya's nature is perhaps most clearly revealed. She combines not only life and death, but also different ideas of the afterlife and the meaning of an honorable death. Her position as ruler over half of the fallen warriors makes her a central figure in the Norse understanding of fate after death.

The archaeological findings of recent decades have significantly expanded our understanding of Freya's role in the cult of the dead. Particularly revealing are the findings of cemeteries that show a combination of martial and cultic elements. This material evidence supports the literary sources and shows the practical significance of Freya in the burial culture of the Norse peoples.

THE MANY NAMES OF FREYA

The multitude of names and epithets Freya bears is more than just poetic embellishment -- it reflects the various aspects of her nature and her far-reaching significance in Norse culture. Snorri Sturluson lists several of these names in his Edda, each of which illuminates a particular facet of the goddess.

The variety of names in Norse mythology follows a complex system of poetic and religious meanings. Each name can be understood as a key to a particular aspect of the deity. In the case of Freya, this diversity of names is particularly pronounced and testifies to her multi-layered role in the religious life of the Norse peoples.

Mardöll, one of her most important epithets, is controversial in its exact translation. One possible interpretation is "the one who illuminates the sea" or "the golden one", which could indicate her connection to splendor and beauty. Other interpretations see a connection to the sea, which would reflect her descent from the sea god Njord.

The name Hörn, which is also used for Freya, could refer to "flax" or "linen". This connection to textile raw materials could point to her role as the patron goddess of domestic activities. Other interpretations see in this name a connection to the Old Norse word for "horn", possibly indicating ritual drinking ceremonies.

Linguistic research has shown that the name Hörn also appears in various place names, especially in connection with places of worship. This geographical distribution of the name provides important clues to the regional distribution of certain aspects of their worship. Archaeological finds at such sites have often shown a connection to textile processing and domestic cults.

Gefn or Gefjon, which can be translated as "the giver", emphasizes Freya's generous and fertile nature. This name emphasizes her role as the goddess of abundance and plenty. The connection between giving and fertility is a common motif in Norse mythology.

The ritual use of these different names is particularly fascinating. Different names were used depending on the type of invocation and the desired aspect of their power. This practice shows a deep understanding of the different manifestations of divine power and the importance of correct invocation in ritual contexts.

The name Syr, which simply means "sow", is particularly interesting. What may seem strange at first glance gains significance when you consider the central role of the pig as a symbol of fertility in Germanic culture. This name links Freya directly with her companion animal Hildesvingi and emphasizes her function as a fertility goddess.

The title Vanadis refers to her as 'Dis of the vanir'. The Disen were female deities or divine beings, and this name emphasizes both Freya's affiliation with the vanir and her position as a powerful female deity. It is one of the names that most directly expresses her divine origins.

Anthropological research has shown that the different names may also reflect different temporal layers of religious development. Some names appear to be older and indicate more primal functions of the goddess, while others may represent later developments or regional variants.

According to tradition, Freya took on various names on her travels. This variety of names could indicate different local cults and forms of worship. The ability to take on different names and thus different aspects fits in with her role as a versatile goddess.

The poetic paraphrases in skaldic poetry add further facets. When gold is described as "Freya's tears", a complex image emerges that combines beauty, wealth and mourning. Such kenningar (poetic paraphrases) contribute to the complexity of her image.

Comparative religious studies have revealed interesting parallels between Freya's multiplicity of names and similar phenomena in other cultures. The practice of assigning different names to one deity is found in many Indo-European religions and points to a common understanding of the various aspects of divine power.

Some of her names also have geographical references. Various place names in Scandinavia, which contain elements such as "Freya" or her other names, testify to the wide spread of her cult. These place names form a kind of sacred geography that reflects the importance of the goddess in everyday life.

The use of different names in different contexts could also indicate different functions of the goddess. As the goddess of war, who receives half of the fallen, she has different names than in her role as goddess of love or magician.

The variety of names also reflects the different traditions from which the cult of Freya may have developed. Some names could refer to older, local goddesses who have merged with Freya over time.

Historical-critical analysis of the various names has shown that they often reflect social and cultural developments. While some names refer to her function as a fertility goddess, others point to her later role as a goddess of the ruling class. This development shows how the cult of Freya changed with society and integrated new aspects.

The significance of these various names goes beyond mere designations -- they are keys to understanding the various aspects and functions of the goddess. Taken as a whole, they paint a picture of a complex deity whose influence extended across many areas of life and religion.

The linguistic study of the names also reveals interesting connections to other Germanic and Indo-European languages. These linguistic links provide clues to the original meaning and function of the goddess as well as to cultural contacts and influences in early Germanic history.

The multitude of names makes Freya one of the most multifaceted goddesses of the Norse pantheon and underlines her central importance in the religious imagination of the Germanic peoples.

FREYA AND FRIGG

CONNECTIONS AND DIFFERENCES

The relationship between Freya and Frigg is one of the most fascinating aspects of Norse mythology. The two most powerful goddesses of the Norse pantheon have such remarkable similarities that the theory has arisen that they may originally have been a single goddess who evolved into two separate figures over time.

The historical development of this possible division is of particular interest to religious history. The earliest sources, especially the reports by Roman authors on Germanic tribes, usually mention only one great goddess. This observation supports the thesis that the differentiation into two distinct goddesses was a later developmental step, possibly caused by social changes in the Germanic world.

The etymological relationship between their names is revealing. "Frigg" is related to the Old High German "frî" (free, to love), while "Freya" means "mistress". Both names indicate high social positions and a connection to love. In various Germanic dialects, there are forms of names that seem to oscillate between the two goddess names - a possible linguistic indication of their original unity.

The thesis of an original identity is supported by further parallels. Both goddesses have magical falcon robes, both are associated with spinning and weaving, and both have husbands who are often on journeys - Odr with Freya, Odin with Frigg. The similarity of the names Odr and Odin reinforces the impression of a possible original unity.

The archaeological findings add a material dimension to this discussion. At many cult sites, there is evidence of the worship of a female deity whose attributes could be attributed to both Freya and Frigg. These overlaps in material culture could indicate an original unity or at least a close connection between the two goddesses.

Nevertheless, there are clear differences between the goddesses. While Frigg appears as the goddess of marriage and domestic order, Freya embodies freer forms of love and sexuality. Frigg is usually portrayed in her role as Odin's wife and mother of Baldr, while Freya appears more independent and self-reliant. These different characterizations could reflect different social developments and social norms.

The different origins of the goddesses are also significant. Frigg belongs to the Aesir, while Freya is a Wanin. This could explain why they were worshipped as separate deities despite their similarities - they could represent different cultural and religious traditions that were merged over time.

The magical abilities of both goddesses differ in their nature. While Freya is associated with Seidr magic, Frigg is associated more with prophetic powers and knowledge of fate. These different magical specializations may have arisen from the splitting of originally united aspects.

One interesting aspect is the different emphasis placed on her worship in different regions and time periods. While Frigg appears more prominently in older continental Germanic sources, Freya is more prominent in the later Scandinavian traditions. This could indicate regional developments and different religious traditions.

The different forms of worship are particularly revealing. Frigg was worshipped more in the official cult and in connection with the institution of marriage, while Freya's cult appears to be freer and more popular. These different cult forms could reflect the social development and increasing institutionalization of religion.

The archaeological finds clearly show these differences in cult practice. While Frigg sanctuaries are often associated with official cult sites and centers of power, Freya cult sites are more frequently found in natural environments and in places associated with popular religiosity.

The relationship between Freya and Frigg remains one of the most interesting mysteries of Norse mythology. Current research tends to take a more nuanced view, considering both the possibility of an original unity and the independent development of both goddesses. The complexity of their relationship possibly reflects the multi-layered religious and social developments in the Germanic world.

CULTS AND WORSHIP IN SCANDINAVIA

The worship of Freya in Scandinavia has left clear traces in archaeological and toponymic records. In Sweden and Norway in particular, there are numerous references to sanctuaries and places of worship dedicated to the goddess.

The geographical distribution of the Freya cult sites follows interesting patterns. Many sanctuaries were located at prominent points in the landscape, such as hills, springs or forest clearings. This connection to the natural environment underlines Freya's origin as a goddess of the vanir and her deep connection to the forces of nature. Archaeological research has shown that many of these cult sites were used for centuries, indicating a remarkable continuity in religious practice.

One particularly important piece of evidence is the discovery of the grave of a presumed Freya priestess in Sweden. The buried woman wore rich jewelry and amulets associated with the goddess. The rich grave furnishings and the careful burial indicate a high social status, which underlines the importance of the Freya cult.

Place name research provides further important clues. Names containing elements such as "Freya", "Fröja" or related terms are frequently found in Scandinavia. The various combinations and compounds are particularly revealing. "Freyslundr" (Freya's grove) refers to sacred forests, "Freysvin" (Freya's meadow) to outdoor sacrificial sites, while "Freyshof" refers to cult buildings. The distribution of these place names allows conclusions to be drawn about the geographical spread of their cult.

The ritual practice in the Freya cult shows a remarkable diversity. In addition to the large public festivals, which were often linked to the seasons and agricultural cycles, there were also private ritual acts. Archaeological finds of domestic altars and small cult figures indicate that

Freya was also worshipped in the domestic sphere. This dual structure - public and private cult - was characteristic of her worship.

The sacrificial practices in the Freya cult can be partially reconstructed through archaeological finds. Various types of offerings have been found at cult sites: Jewelry, especially made of gold and silver, but also animal sacrifices and food. The finds indicate that the offerings were often related to the various aspects of the goddess - precious metals for the goddess of wealth, fruit and crops for the goddess of fertility.

The references to female cult leaders are particularly interesting. The sources speak of priestesses who acted in Freya's name and possibly also carried out magical practices. This religious leadership role of women is remarkable for medieval Scandinavian society and could point to older matriarchal traditions.

The archaeological findings show a clear development of cult practices over the centuries. While earlier finds often point to natural sanctuaries and simple sacrificial sites, more complex temple complexes are also found in the later Viking Age. This development possibly reflects the increasing institutionalization of religion. Particularly interesting are finds of buildings that combined both cultic and secular functions, indicating the close connection between religion and everyday life.

Seasonal festivals played an important role in the worship of Freya. Spring and fertility festivals in particular are likely to have been associated with her cult. Archaeological finds at cult sites often show traces of regular festive activities, such as fireplaces for ritual meals or platforms for ceremonial acts. Some of these festive traditions may have survived in a Christianized form, as folkloristic studies suggest.

The geographical distribution of the cult evidence shows interesting patterns. While in Scandinavia, especially in Sweden and Norway, there is a great deal of evidence of Freya worship, there is little evidence of this in the southern Germanic region. This could indicate regional differences in religious tradition.

The importance of the cult of Freya for everyday life is reflected in various archaeological finds. Small amulets and household shrines show that the worship of the goddess was not limited to large temples, but also played an important role in the private sphere. Particularly interesting are finds of ritual objects in homes, which point to domestic cult practices.

The material culture of the Freya cult also included ritual implements and cult objects. Archaeological finds of special robes, staffs and other ritual objects provide an insight into the practice of Freya worship. Of particular interest are finds of spindles and loom weights, which may indicate ritual activities in connection with textile work.

Christianization meant the end of public Freya worship, but some elements may have survived in folk customs and folklore. In particular, customs related to love, fertility and domestic happiness sometimes show parallels with aspects of the Freya cult.

The transformation of religious practices during Christianization is particularly revealing. Many elements of the Freya cult were not simply eradicated, but transformed into new forms. Sacred places were often converted into Christian churches, sometimes even incorporating architectural elements of the old sanctuaries. Certain rituals and festive customs were also continued in a Christian reinterpretation.

This archaeological and historical evidence shows that the worship of Freya was deeply rooted in Scandinavian society. It encompassed both public acts of worship and private piety and had a lasting impact on religious life until Christianization.

In recent decades, modern archaeological research has considerably expanded our understanding of the Freya cult through new methods and finds. In particular, the analysis of settlement structures and cult sites has shown how closely the worship of the goddess was linked to people's everyday lives.

THE SUEBI ISIS

A POSSIBLE CONNECTION

One of the most interesting theories on Freya's origins relates to an enigmatic goddess mentioned by the Roman historian Tacitus in his "Germania": "Isis", who was worshipped by the Suebi. This connection could provide important clues to the early development of the Freya cult and its possible continental Germanic roots.

The historical classification of this Suebi isis poses particular challenges for researchers. The Suebi of the first century AD were a tribal confederation that extended over large parts of Central Europe. Their religious practices have come down to us mainly through Roman sources, which makes interpretation even more difficult. Tacitus' description must therefore be seen in the context of the Roman perception of Germanic religiosity.

Tacitus reports on a cult among the Suebi, a Germanic tribe that worshipped a goddess whom he identifies with the Egyptian Isis. The symbol of this deity that he mentions is particularly striking: a ship. This description takes on particular significance when compared with Freya's hall Sessrumnir, which is described as both a building and a ship.

However, Tacitus' interpretation must be viewed critically. As a Roman observer, he tended to equate foreign deities with known Roman or, in this case, Egyptian gods. This interpretatio romana can provide important clues, but may also conceal essential aspects of the original Germanic deity.

Recent archaeological research has provided interesting findings to support Tacitus' reports. In various Suebian settlement areas, cult sites have been discovered that show evidence of the worship of a female deity. Finds of representations of ships and ritual objects associated with water and fertility are particularly revealing.

The meaning of the ship symbol is particularly interesting. In Germanic culture, ships played an important role in the cult of the dead, as evidenced by the well-known ship burials. This connection between the ship and the cult of the dead fits in with Freya's later role as goddess of the dead, who receives half of the fallen warriors in her hall.

Another significant aspect is the geographical spread of the cult described by Tacitus. The Suebi settled in an area that stretched from the Baltic Sea to central Germany. This region could have played an important role in the transmission of religious ideas between the continental Germanic and Scandinavian regions.

The temporal dimension is also worth noting. Tacitus' report dates back to the first century AD, several centuries before Norse mythology was written down. The goddess he describes could represent an early form of a female deity who later differentiated into various goddesses such as Freya and Frigg.

Alternative theories also see parallels between the Suebian Isis and other Germanic goddesses such as Nerthus or Nehalennia. Nehalennia in particular, who was worshipped on the North Sea coast and was also associated with ships, is often seen as a possible link between the Suebian Isis and later Germanic goddesses.

The ritual practices described by Tacitus provide further clues. He mentions religious festivals and processions in which the ship symbol played a central role. Archaeological finds confirm the existence of such ritual practices. Remains of processional routes and ritual platforms were discovered at various sites, indicating complex ritual acts.

The function of the ship as a religious symbol goes beyond the pure cult of the dead. Ships also symbolized fertility, trade and prosperity -- aspects that were later also reflected in the nature of Freya. The connection between death and fertility, which is characteristic of Freya, could already have been present in this early cult.

A direct equation of the Suebian Isis with Freya would certainly be too simplistic. More likely is a complex development process in which various religious traditions and concepts of God merged with one another. The parallels between the Suebian Isis described by Tacitus and Freya suggest a possible connection, even if this cannot be clearly proven.

Comparative religious studies reveal interesting parallels between the Suebi cult practices described and later Scandinavian rituals. In particular, the use of processional barques and ritual ship representations can be found in both traditions. This continuity could indicate common religious roots.

The significance of Tacitus' report lies above all in the fact that it provides a rare contemporary insight into the religious ideas of the continental Germanic tribes. The parallels to later Nordic traditions could indicate long lines of continuity in the development of Germanic religion.

The possible connection between the Suebian Isis and Freya shows how complex the development of religious ideas can be. It warns us to be wary of overly simple equations, but also points to possible lines of development that led to the later cult of Freya.

FREYA'S LEGACY IN GERMANIC CULTURE

The impact of the Freya cult on Germanic culture extends far beyond the time of her active worship. Its traces can be found in language, customs and cultural traditions, some of which have survived to the present day.

Linguistic research has shown how profound Freya's influence was on the development of the Germanic languages. The etymological connection between her name and central terms such as "woman", "free" and "Friday" testifies to her fundamental importance for the Germanic world view. The development of the word "Frau", which originally had a sacred meaning and emphasized the divine dignity of the female sphere, is particularly revealing.

A particularly clear example of Freya's cultural heritage can be found in the German language. The term "Frau" (woman) goes back etymologically to the same root word as the name Freya. This linguistic connection shows how deeply rooted the idea of Freya as the archetype of the feminine was in Germanic culture. The name "Freitag" is also associated with Freya by some researchers.

Various motifs can be found in medieval literature that may have their origins in Freya. Elements reminiscent of aspects of the Freya cult appear particularly in courtly minned poetry. The idea of the transformative power of love and the connection between love and gold are motifs with parallels to Freya's mythology.

The literary transformation of Freya in the Middle Ages is particularly revealing. While direct references to the pagan goddess were avoided, many of her attributes lived on in literary figures and motifs. Courtly literature developed a complex system of ideas of love and images of women that clearly parallels Freya's various aspects. The combination of love, beauty and magical power, for example, can be found in many medieval tales.

Folkloric research has shown that various customs and traditions may have their origins in the worship of Freya. Wedding customs and fertility rituals in particular sometimes show elements reminiscent of the cult of Freya. The special significance of certain animals, such as cats, in folkloristic traditions could be partly due to the connection with Freya.

The continuity of certain ritual practices into the Christian era is particularly interesting. Many customs associated with love, marriage and fertility show striking parallels to traditional elements of the Freya cult. The transformation of these practices under Christian influence provides important insights into the adaptability of religious ideas.

Although Christianization led to the end of the official worship of Freya, some of her aspects may have been integrated into Christian holy figures. Figures of the Virgin Mary in particular sometimes took on functions that had previously been attributed to Freya. This can be seen, for example, in Mary's role as the protector of home and family.

The transformation of religious symbols during Christianization is particularly revealing. Many symbols associated with Freya were transferred to a Christian context. For example, sacred places associated with Freya were often rededicated as Marian pilgrimage sites. Certain attributes of Freya, such as her connection to medicinal herbs and her protective function, can also be found in the worship of the Virgin Mary.

In the visual arts of the Middle Ages and the early modern period, motifs can occasionally be found that could go back to pre-Christian ideas of goddesses. In particular, depictions of female figures with cats or in connection with gold and jewelry could be influenced by Freya traditions.

The artistic reception of Freya shows an interesting development. While direct depictions of the pagan goddess were avoided, some of her attributes lived on in Christian iconography. This is particularly evident in the depiction of female saints and allegorical female figures.

The Nordic Renaissance in the 19th century led to a revival of interest in Freya. Romantic artists and poets took up the figure of the Norse goddess of love and reinterpreted her in the spirit of their time. This reception played a significant role in shaping the modern image of Freya.

The Romantic rediscovery of Norse mythology led to an intensive artistic exploration of Freya. In painting, literature and music, she was portrayed as a symbol of primal Nordic femininity. This interpretation often reflected the longings and ideals of the 19th century more than historical realities.

In 19th and early 20th century literature, Freya was often portrayed as a symbol of original Nordic femininity. This interpretation reflected the contemporary search for national identity and "Germanic roots", but must be viewed critically from today's perspective.

The naming also shows Freya's enduring cultural heritage. The name "Freya" and its variants are still used as a first name today, especially in Scandinavian countries. Traces of Freya worship have also been preserved in toponymy.

Traditional customs and folk festivals sometimes still contain elements that may go back to Freya. Spring festivals and wedding customs in particular may have retained relics of old Freya traditions, even if this connection cannot always be clearly proven.

Modern research has examined the continuity of certain cultural practices in detail. This has shown that many supposedly "old" traditions are often the result of later interpretations and new creations. Nevertheless, authentic links to pre-Christian rituals can be proven in some customs.

The cultural after-effects of Freya show how religious ideas can continue to have an effect even after the end of her active worship. Elements of the Freya cult live on in various cultural areas in a transformed form.

Freya's legacy in Germanic culture is therefore a complex web of direct traditions, transformed elements and later interpretations. The scientific analysis of these different layers enables a better understanding of both the historical worship of Freya and its cultural repercussions up to the present day.

MODERN INTERPRETATIONS AND MEANING

The significance of Freya today is revealed through various scientific and social interpretations. As a complex mythological figure, she offers many points of reference for modern discourses and interpretations.

Feminist research in recent decades has contributed to a new understanding of Freya's role in Norse mythology. Her position as a powerful female deity, ruling over both traditionally 'feminine' domains such as love and fertility and 'masculine' domains such as war and death, is seen as an example of a more complex understanding of gender roles in pre-Christian times. These interpretations have significantly expanded the earlier, often simplistic image of Freya as a pure goddess of love and fertility.

In modern religious studies, Freya is seen as a key figure for understanding pre-Christian social structures. Her position as a powerful female deity who rules over both "feminine" aspects such as love and fertility and traditionally "masculine" areas such as war and death offers important insights into historical concepts of gender.

Feminist research has dealt intensively with Freya. Her portrayal as a self-determined, sexually autonomous figure who successfully resists unwanted appropriation makes her an interesting reference figure for modern discussions about female self-determination. In particular, her refusal to be forced into marriage by the giants is interpreted as an early example of female resistance to patriarchal structures.

Anthropological research sees Freya as an important example of the complexity of pre-Christian concepts of God. The combination of seemingly contradictory aspects in her person - such as love and death, fertility and war - is seen as an indication of a more holistic view of the world. This integration of different areas of life in one divine figure stands in contrast to later, more polarized religious ideas.

In psychology, especially in Jungian approaches, Freya is interpreted as an archetype of various aspects of the feminine. Her combination of love, death and transformation makes her a complex figure who can symbolize various psychological development processes. The unification of apparent opposites in her person is interpreted as a symbol of psychological wholeness.

Modern mythology research sees Freya as an interesting example of the development and transformation of religious ideas. The various theories about her origins show the complexity of religious development processes and the difficulty of separating historical truth from later interpretation.

The ecological movement has taken up Freya's connection to nature. As a vanir goddess with her close relationship to natural cycles, she is sometimes seen as a symbol of a more harmonious relationship between humans and nature. Her various animal aspects are interpreted in this context as an expression of the interconnectedness of all life.

In gender research, Freya is studied as an example of the construction and transformation of gender roles. Her combination of various characteristics traditionally categorized as male or female is seen as an indication of the historical relativity of gender concepts.

Sociological research examines the significance of Freya for the understanding of pre-modern social structures. Her various functions as a goddess of love, war and death provide insights into the complex organization of early Germanic societies.

Religious studies research looks at Freya in the context of comparative religious studies. Parallels to other Indo-European goddesses shed light on common cultural roots and lines of development of various religious traditions.

The enduring scholarly fascination with Freya is due not least to her complexity. As a figure who unites various aspects of human experience, she offers numerous starting points for modern interpretations and analyses.

Freya's significance for the understanding of historical processes is unbroken. Her story exemplifies the transformation of religious ideas over time and the enduring relevance of mythological figures for understanding cultural developments.

Freya is also attracting increasing attention in modern popular culture. She is being reinterpreted as a complex mythological figure in literature, film and other media. These contemporary adaptations help to keep interest in Norse mythology alive and open up new perspectives on ancient traditions.

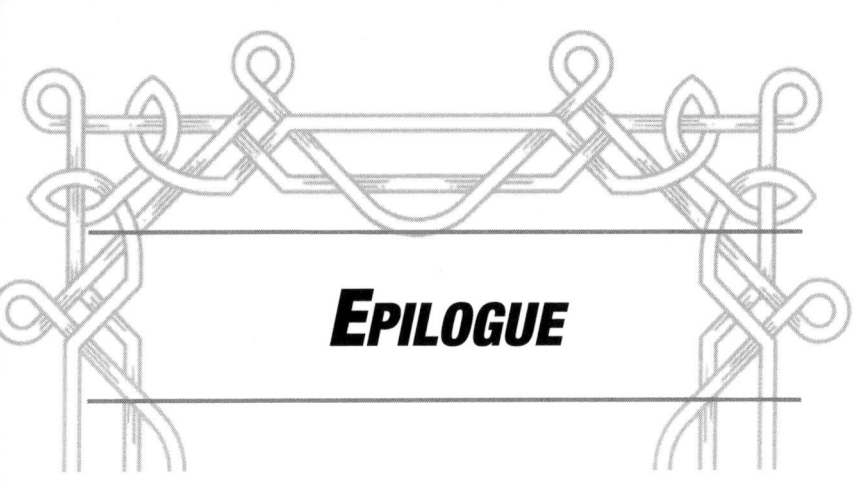

EPILOGUE

The journey through the various aspects and levels of meaning of the goddess Freya reveals the extraordinary complexity of this mythological figure. What began as an investigation of a Norse deity developed into an exploration of fundamental questions about religion, society and the human psyche.

The complexity of Freya reflects the complexity of human experience. It unites aspects that are often perceived as contradictory: Love and war, life and death, magic and everyday life. This union of opposites makes her a timelessly fascinating figure who is still able to appeal to modern people.

The development of Freya's reception over the centuries is particularly remarkable. From the powerful goddess of Norse mythology through various transformations in medieval and modern culture to modern interpretations, her enduring significance as a symbol of female power and self-determination is evident.

Scientific research into the Freya cult has not only broadened our understanding of Nordic religion, but has also provided important insights into the development of religious ideas and social structures. The various theories on its origin and development show the complexity of religious and cultural transformation processes.

There are various promising prospects for the future of Freya research. New archaeological finds could provide further insights into the historical practice of her worship. The investigation of her role in different cultural contexts promises deeper insights into the significance of female deities for social developments.

Freya's enduring presence in art, literature and popular culture shows her unbroken relevance as a symbol and projection screen for human hopes, fears and longings. Her various aspects offer points of reference for modern discourses on gender roles, power and spiritual development.

At a time when traditional gender roles and power structures are increasingly being questioned, Freya is gaining new significance as an example of a complex, self-determined female figure. Her story shows that alternative ideas of femininity and power have a long historical tradition.

The study of Freya also teaches us something about the nature of religious and cultural tradition. How a deity can take on different meanings over the centuries and still retain its fundamental fascination shows the dynamic nature of cultural symbols and their ability to adapt to new contexts.

The story of Freya is therefore not just a chapter in Norse mythology, but a living example of the enduring importance of mythological figures in human culture. It reflects the timeless search for understanding and meaning that connects people from all eras.An epilogue is very similar to a prologue, but it occurs at the end of your story, though usually separate from the main plot. It might offer a glimpse of the future to share a sense of closure with your readers, or entice them to read the next in a series or collection.

Similar to the prologue, the epilogue should be placed in the main body content of your book and is therefore not technically back matter.

GLOSSARY

Aesir: The main group of Norse gods, including Odin, Thor and Tyr. In contrast to the vanir, they are associated with war, order and rule.

Brisingamen: Freya's famous necklace, created by four dwarves. It is considered the most beautiful piece of jewelry in the world and is a symbol of her power and beauty.

Dis (pl. Disen): Female deities or divine beings in Norse mythology. Freya is also known as Vanadis.

Edda: Collection of Old Norse literature containing important sources on Norse mythology. Consists of the Elder (Song) Edda and the Younger (Prose) Edda by Snorri Sturluson.

Falcon robe: Freya's magical garment that allows her to transform into a falcon.

Frigg: Wife of Odin and queen of Asgard. Shows many parallels to Freya and could originally have been the same deity.

Gefn: One of Freya's names, means "the giver" and emphasizes her aspect as the goddess of abundance.

Gullveig: Mysterious figure whose burning triggered the war between the Aesir and the vanir. Possibly another name for Freya.

Hildesvini: Freya's wild boar, whose name means "fighting boar" and symbolizes her connection to fertility.

Hnoss: daughter of Freya and Odr, whose name means "jewel" or "treasure".

Hörn: One of Freya's names, possibly associated with "flax" or ritual drinking ceremonies.

LokAesirna: Eddic poem in which Loki mocks all the gods, including Freya.

Mardöll: One of Freya's names, possibly meaning "the one who illuminates the sea".

Nehalennia: Germanic goddess who was worshipped on the North Sea coast and possibly has connections to Freya.

Njord: Freya's father, god of the sea and seafaring, belongs to the vanir.

Odr: Freya's husband, who often travels and whose absence she mourns.

Ragnarök: the twilight of the gods, the final battle in Norse mythology.

Seidr: Form of magic that is particularly associated with Freya and which she also taught Odin.

Sessrumnir: Freya's hall in Asgard, whose name means "the one with many seats" and which also appears as a ship.

Scaldic poetry: a form of Nordic poetry in which gold is often referred to as "Freya's tears".

Suebian Isis: Germanic goddess mentioned by Tacitus, possibly an early form of Freya.

Syr: One of Freya's names, means "sow" and refers to her connection to pigs as fertility symbols.

Thrym: Giant prince who stole Thor's hammer and demanded Freya as his bride.

Vanadis: Freya's title, means "Dis (divine woman) of the vanir".

Vanaheim: Home of the vanir, one of the nine worlds in Norse cosmology.

Vanir: Group of fertility gods to which Freya belongs. Known for their connection to nature and magic.

Valhall: Odin's hall, where half of the fallen warriors go, while the other half go to Freya.

Volkwang: Freya's realm in Asgard, meaning "field of the people" or "field of the army".

Ynglinga saga: Historical saga by Snorri Sturluson, which contains important information about Freya.

Dwarves: Mythical creatures and skilled craftsmen who created the Brisingamen for Freya.

Made in the USA
Monee, IL
09 April 2025

15500578R00066